To the
Heavenly Rose

Project Directors: Margaret L. Kaplan, John K. Crowley

Designer: Carol A. Robson

Library of Congress Cataloging-in-Publication Data

Parker, Carolyn
    The poetry of roses / selected and photographed by Carolyn Parker.
        p.   cm.
    ISBN 0–8109–3736–0
    I. Roses—Poetry.   I. Title.
PN6110.R6P27   1995
808.81'936—dc20   94-42121

Published in 1995 by Harry N. Abrams, Incorporated, New York
A Times Mirror Company

Printed and bound in Hong Kong

ʹForeword

Artists use the objects of the universe as inspiration, image, and symbol. From antiquity, offerings of roses have appeared in literature. All aspects of the bountiful bush—roots, stems, thorns, leaves, petals, stamens, corollas—have been described in numberless ways. The flower—in bud, half opened, fully open, finally withered or even invisible—has been a subject. On the following pages the rose symbolizes love, life, death, the sun, the heart, the soul, and perfection.

The rose is nature's most precious gift: beauty, friendship, grace, nectar, fragrance, silence. My breath has often been taken away by the sight of luxurious quantities of roses in my garden, or by the details of ecstatic opening, glimpsed through the lens of my camera. The golden pens of the poets in this book have had the same effect. I share the feelings of Rilke, when he wrote in *The Roses,* "I breathe you in as if you were all of life."

It was a great privilege to immerse myself in the wisdom of the ages in search of rose poems. There were hundreds to choose from, and I know there are many more being written even at this moment. I searched the garden each day for single remarkable blooms, or for armfuls to play with and to photograph—to capture, as Hafiz says, this "heart-enchanting" flower. Please join me in this celebration of the poetry of roses.

CAROLYN PARKER

LAFAYETTE, CALIFORNIA

Thank You

First of all I want to thank John Crowley at Abrams for loving my photos and Margaret Kaplan for suggesting this beautiful project to me, special gratitude goes to designer Carol Robson for her sensitive use of my photography in bringing the visual essence of Rose poetry to these pages. Thank you Susie Kohl, Collins Flannery, and Sidney Davenport for invaluable help in the beginning stages. Thank you Marilyn McGivney and Gay Montandon for sharing your libraries with me. Thank you Rachel Dacus for your thoughts, words, and ideas. Special thanks to David Israel for your scholarship, great sense of history, and wonderful suggestions. Thank you so much, Amy Peterson, for your computer expertise with preliminary planning.

Thank you to the translators: Stephen Mitchell, Edward Snow, and Al Poulin for your devotion to Rainer Maria Rilke's poetry and for your contributions to this book. Thank you Robert Bly, Alan S. Trueblood, Robert Hass, Pat Tarnapol, Ron Duce, David Lawson, Indran Amirthanayagam, John Italia, and Richard Deane for contributions in these pages. Special thanks to Willis Barnstone for your generous contributions.

Thank you Sheila Maher for giving me red roses when I did not have enough.

Thank you, in memory, to Ivy O. Duce, who told me the name of my business really should be "Fleur." Thank you, Barbara Brustman, for endless ribbons and laces, and thank you to my "Flower Brother" Bhau Kalchuri.

Loving thanks to my artist husband Leroy Parker, whose ceramic vessels appear in many photos and who was always willing to paint a new backdrop for me. Thank you, my darling daughters Anna and Oneita Parker, for your unfailing encouragement.

Thank you, especially, to Dr. James MacKie, for inspiration and guidance throughout this project.

In the garden mystery glows
the secret is hidden in the rose

Farid ud-Din Attar, 1119–1230

That one adorned the beauty of the rose garden
who vanished like a rose in the soul of a thorn.

Mystical Poems of Rumi, Jalaluddin Rumi, 1207–1273

The Nightingale now trills his love-song to the rose;
And when she feigns disdain, his plaint the louder grows.
   Then he begins his pretty quips and pleasantries,
Until her sugar-laden lips in smiles unclose.

See how that happy rose in this fair garden blows!
Anon the clouds shed tears—anon there laughs the rose!
   Yon cypress is the bond-slave of the rose, e'en though
She boasts she's free because in stately pride she grows.

The new wine of the rose-tree of our Youth is love!
The Capital of everlasting Life is Love!
   Water of Life dost seek, like hoary Khizar? Know
The fountain of that sweet life-giving stream is—LOVE!

Hafiz Meditates in His Rose Garden, Hafiz, 1300–1388

My garden all is overblown with roses,
My spirit all is overblown with rhyme,
As like a drunken honeybee I waver
From house to garden and again to house
And, undetermined which delight to favour
On verse and rose alternately carouse.

Sonnet, Vita Sackville-West, 1892–1962

With no recourse
She shines, fresh from the shower,
Webbed in diamonds,
Lustrous in the morning dew.

Roots delirious in mineral mud,
Companion to the neighboring bud
And withered blossom leaving,
She is the daughter of the one
Who shapes the roseate puffs of cloud,
A silent shimmering vision of gold
Expanding in the blue mandala evening.

When you breathe her fragrance
The moonbeams sing
The chorus of Orion's symphony,
The spinning song of nebulae—
Unfolding petals, petals unfolding
The radiant face of beauty.

The Carolina Rose, David Lawson, born 1936

Would Jove appoint some flower to reign
In matchless beauty on the plain
The Rose (Mankind will all agree)
The Rose the Queen of Flowers should be.

Sappho, sixth century B.C.

This bud of love, by
summer's ripening breath
May prove a beauteous
flower when next we meet

Romeo and Juliet, William Shakespeare, 1564–1616

Rose, your majesty—once, to the ancients, you were
Just a calyx with the simplest of rims.
But for us, you are the full, the numberless flower,
the inexhaustible countenance.

In your wealth you seem to be wearing gown upon gown
upon a body of nothing but light;
yet each separate petal is at the same time the negation
of all clothing and the refusal of it.

Your fragrance has been calling its sweetest names
in our direction, for hundreds of years;
suddenly it hangs in the air like fame.

Even so, we have never known what to call it; we guess . . .
And memory is filled with it unawares
which we prayed for from hours that belong to us.

The Sonnets to Orpheus, VI, Rainer Maria Rilke, 1875–1926

Amid a mild rain, the air still humid,
I stroll awhile down into Rock Creek Park
The rose has lost her petals: now perfumèd
shall be the dust with memory's tender mark

Sitting to jot these words the ink gets bleared
although I crouch beneath a lighted eave
One notices that youth has disappeared
yet beauty still is glistening at one's sleeve

Summer Saunter, David Raphael Israel, born 1956

18

In the last month of May
   I made her posies;
I heard her often say
   That she loved roses.

English, seventeenth century

Roses on a brier,
Pearls from out the bitter sea,
Such is earth's desire
    However pure it be.

Neither bud nor brier,
    Neither pearl nor brine for me:
Be stilled, my long desire;
    There shall be no more sea.

Be stilled, my passionate heart;
    Old earth shall end, new earth shall be:
Be still, and earn thy part
    Where shall be no more sea.

Roses on a Brier, Christina Rossetti, 1830 1894

I can charm that man
I can cause him to become fascinated

What are you saying to me?
I am dressed in colors of the roses?
and as beautiful as the roses?

I can make him bashful
I do wonder what can be the matter with him
that he is bashful?

I can do this where he may be
under the earth
or in the very center of the earth!

Love-Charm Song, Traditional American Indian,
Ojibwa Tribe

Your skin a taste
of roses, shiver
of flame.

John Italia, born 1948

Kissing your lips
I try to forget roses

The Kiss, Indran Amirthanayagam, born 1960

The red rose whispers of passion,
    And the white rose breathes of love;
O, the red rose is a falcon,
    And the white rose is a dove.

But I send you a cream-white rosebud
    With a flush on its petal tips;
For the love that is purest and sweetest
    Has a kiss of desire on the lips.

A White Rose, John Boyle O'Reilly, 1844–1890

Strange to weave gardenias for your mantle
When you are a rose.
We held them in both hands, closed our eyes
And breathed in your absence,
Our new symbol of death.
How lasting their fragrance!

But you are a rose,
And gardenias are waxen shadows of roses.
Roses have hidden golden eyes that look to the sun.
Full of Eros, Agape and Sophia,
They place their silken petals just so!
Their being is silence.

And even I, walking barefoot in the garden,
Even I don't know them. They take my smiles
Against their milky bosoms, all my gratitude to you
Whose heart is an open rose,
Whose rose is white as gardenias,
Whose presence outlasts the night.

Elegy, September Ninth, Gay Montandon, born 1943

un(bee)mo

vi
n(in)g
are(th
e)you(o
nly)

asl(rose)eep

un(bee)mo, e.e. cummings, 1894–1962

Nobody knows this little Rose—
It might a pilgrim be
Did I not take it from the ways
And lift it up to thee.
Only a Bee will miss it—
Only a Butterfly,
Hastening from far journey—
On its breast to lie—
Only a Bird will wonder—
Only a Breeze will sigh—
Ah Little Rose—how easy
For such as thee to die!

Emily Dickinson, 1830–1886

My roses in this jungle
    Which assaults me every day
Give me solace, love, and comfort
    For moments world at bay

When I tend them sympathetically
    And minister their needs
Raiment is a blush of Grace
    Seduction without weeds

Incidental Miracles, Ron Duce, born 1945

    Rose
Unbent by winds, unchill'd by snows,
    Far from the winters of the west,
    By every breeze and season blest,
    Returns the sweets by nature given
    In softest incense back to Heaven. . . .

George Gordon, Lord Byron, 1788–1824

I was a child. I remember
gathering wild roses.
They had so many thorns—
I didn't want to break them—
I believed they were buds
and were going to flower.

Then I met you. O love,
you had so many thorns!
I didn't want to strip them—
I believed they would flower.

All this I review today
and smile—smile
and wander the roads
driven by the wind.
I was a child.

Thorns, Lucian Blaga, 1895–1961

I wish I were a scarlet rose
so you might lift me in your hands
and pull me to your snowy breasts.

Byzantine, fourth to sixth century

I sent my love two roses,—one
    As white as driven snow,
And one a blushing royal red,
    A flaming Jacqueminot. . . .

My heart sank when I met her: sure
    I had been overbold,
For on her breast my pale rose lay
    In virgin whiteness cold.

Yet with low words she greeted me,
    With smiles divinely tender;
Upon her cheek the red rose dawned,—
    The white rose meant surrender.

The White Flag, John Hay, 1838–1905

What is more lovely than a flaming rose
That blooms, more felt than seen, within the heart.
With every single act of love, it grows
Until no thing in life remains apart.

Its fragrance laden with a sweet content
Abides, inclusive, interpenetrant.
Light radiates through petals that unfold, unfold
Gently, releasing deeply hidden spirit gold.
Gently, releasing spirit gold.

Roses in splendor blooming,
Their Attar of Beauty
Thrown like a scarf on the bosom of dawn,
Call to those worlds of enchantment and bliss
That soaring and high beyond of the heart
and I perished, a rose among them.

The Flaming Rose, Malcolm Schloss, 1898–1956

Gift of the Roses, Richard Deane, born 1944

Sweet, serene, sky-like flower,
Haste to adorn her bower,
From thy long cloudy bed
Shoot forth thy damask head.

Vermilion ball that's given
From lip to lip in heaven,
Love's couch's coverlet,
Haste, haste to make her bed.

The Rose Bower, Richard Lovelace, 1618–1658

O sweet the rose that blossometh on Friendship's tree!
It fills my heart with joy and ecstasy.
    I seek the rose's company because her scent
Recalls the fragrance sweet of ONE belov'd by me.

Selections from the Rubaiyat and Odes of Hafiz, Hafiz, 1300–1388

Hidden below the stairs
I found roses running wild.
Holding the hose thoughtlessly
on a former flower bed, I was snagged
by their sickly stick canes and uncanny perfume.
No rose grew there before.

Shabby, hardened, they were sustained
on an occasional manna of rain
which they cupped with ragged hands.
Under unyielding suns their knotted trunks
zig-zagged in desperation,
cannibalizing their own blooms.

A heat-crimped rose head
sang to me in a voice
florid as a lady's room.
Its velvet centifolic depth
crawled with insects fine as pencil ticks.
Its blasted eye stared blind
from petals shriveled back,
I never planted a rose there.

In the middle of that wild bed
stood one untortured perfect bud,
a wobbling arrow of biology
thwacked into beauty's bull's eye.
Slowly, over a red canyon of time,
it turned and smiled.
No rose ever looked at me like that.

Encounter, Rachel Dacus, born 1949

The bright rosebuds, these hawthorns shroud
Within their perfumed bower
Have never closed beneath a cloud
Nor bent before a shower—

Had darkness once obscured their sun
Or kind dew turned to rain
No storm-cleared sky that ever shone
Could win such bliss again—

Emily Jane Bronte, 1818–1848

"A rose, but one, none other rose had I,
A rose, one rose, and this was wondrous fair,
One rose, a rose that gladden'd earth and sky,
One rose, my rose, that sweeten'd all mine air—
I cared not for the thorns; the thorns were there.

"One rose, a rose to gather by and by,
One rose, a rose, to gather and to wear,
No rose but one—what other rose had I?
One rose, my rose; a rose that will not die,—
He dies who loves it,—if the worm be there."

Pelleas and Ettarre, Alfred Lord Tennyson, 1809–1892

As late I rambled in the happy fields,
    What time the sky-lark shakes the tremulous dew
    From his lush clover covert;—when anew
Adventurous knights take up their dinted shields:
I saw the sweetest flower wild nature yields,
    A fresh-blown musk-rose; 'twas the first that threw
    Its sweets upon the summer: graceful it grew
As is the wand that queen Titania wields.
And, as I feasted on the fragrancy,
    I thought the garden-rose it far excell'd:
But when, O Wells! thy roses came to me
    My sense with their deliciousness was spell'd:
Soft voices had they, that with tender plea
    Whisper'd of peace, and truth, and friendliness unquell'd.

To a Friend Who Sent Me Some Roses, John Keats, 1795–1821

Didyme plunders me with her beauty.
When I look at her I am wax over fire.
If she's black, what of it? So are coals.
When kindled, they glow like blooming roses.

Askelepiades, flourished c. 270 B.C.

When Heaven Thy features pencill'd, O my
    Mistress fair,
And limn'd each heart-enchanting line of
    beauty there,
   She chose the purple violet for her pen, and
    trac'd
Her work upon a rose's petals unaware!

Selections from the Rubaiyat and Odes of Hafiz, Hafiz, 1300–1388

I wanted this morning to bring you a gift of roses.
But I took so many in my wide belt
The tightened knots could not contain them all

And burst asunder. The roses taking wing
In the wind were all blown out to sea,
Following the water, never to return;

The waves were red with them as if aflame.
This evening my dress bears their perfume still:
You may take from it now their fragrant souvenir.

The Roses of Sa'adi, Marceline Desbordes-Valmore, 1786–1859

And the movement in the roses, look:
gestures from such small angles of deflection
that they'd remain invisible, if their
rays did not fan out into the universe.
Look at that white one which blissfully unfolded
and stands there in the great open petals
like a Venus upright in the seashell;
and the blushing one, which as if confused
turns across to one that is cool,
and how that cold one stands, wrapped in itself,
among the open ones that shed everything.
And *what* they shed: how it can be
light and heavy, a cloak, a burden, a wing
and a mask, it varies endlessly,
and *how* they shed it: as before the loved one.

What can't they be: was that yellow one,
which lies there hollow and open, not the rind
of a fruit, in which the very same yellow,
more collected, orange-redder, was juice?
And was opening-out too much for this one,
since in the air its indescribable pink
took on the bitter aftertaste of violet?
And that cambric one, is it not a dress
in which, still soft and breath-warm, the chemise
clings, both of them cast off at once
in the morning shadows of the old forest pool?
And this one, opalescent porcelain,
fragile, a shallow china cup
and filled with tiny bright butterflies,—
and that one, which contains nothing but itself.

And aren't all that way, containing just themselves,
if self-containing means: to change the world outside
and wind and rain and patience of the spring
and guilt and restlessness and muffled fate
and the darkness of the evening earth
out to the changing and flying and fleeing of the clouds
and the vague influence of distant stars
into a hand full of inwardness.

Now it lies carefree in these open roses.

The Bowl of Roses, Rainer Maria Rilke, 1875–1926

I have a garden of my own,
but so with roses overgrown,
and lilies, that you would it guess
to be a little wilderness.

Andrew Marvell, 1621–1678

Fall back, fall back, fall back,
make way, make way, make way,
the bugles are blowing,
the flageolets piping!
Stars are plunging,
dawns arising.
Lower the lights
let fragrances rise,
troops of jasmine,
spice-pinks, and broom
running,
flying,
pelting,
catching,
with flowers,
with glitter,
with roses,
with flame.

Sor Juana Inés de La Cruz, 1652–1695

43

Like a rose embowered
   In its own green leaves,
By warm winds deflowered,
   Till the scent it gives
Makes faint with too much sweet those
   heavy wingèd thieves.

To a Skylark, Percy Bysshe Shelley, 1792–1822

A Petal shower
of mountain roses,
   and the sound of the rapids.

Matsuo Bashō, 1644–1694

The rose
was not searching for the sunrise:
almost eternal on its branch,
it was searching for something else.

The rose
was not searching for darkness or science:
borderline of flesh and dream,
it was searching for something else.

The rose
was not searching for the rose.
Motionless in the sky
it was searching for something else.

Casida of the Rose, Federico Garcia Lorca, 1895–1936

It was not in the Winter
    Our loving lot was cast;
It was the time of roses—
    We pluck'd them as we pass'd!

That churlish season never frown'd
    On early lovers yet:
O no—the world was newly crown'd
    With flowers when first we met!

'Twas twilight, and I bade you go,
    But still you held me fast;
It was the time of roses—
    We pluck'd them as we pass'd!

Time of Roses, Thomas Hood, 1835–1874

Thou Eglantine, so bright with sunny showers,
Proud as a rainbow spanning half the vale,
Thou one fair shrub, oh! shed thy flowers,
And stir not in the gale.
For thus to see thee nodding in the air,
To see thy arch thus stretch and bend,
Thus rise and thus descend,—
Disturbs me till the sight is more than I can bear.

'Tis Said, That Some Have Died for Love,
William Wordsworth, 1770–1850

I sent thee late a rosy wreath,
Not so much honoring thee,
As giving it a hope, that there
It could not withered be.
But thou thereon did'st only breathe.
And sent'st it back to me;
Since when it grows and smells, I swear,
Not of itself but thee.

To Celia, Ben Jonson, 1572–1637

And the rose like a nymph to the bath addressed,
Which unveiled the depth of her glowing breast,
Till, fold after fold, to the fainting air
The soul of her beauty and love lay bare;

The Sensitive Plant, Percy Bysshe Shelley, 1792–1822

What would the rose with all her pride be worth,
Were there no sun to call her brightness forth?

Love Alone, Thomas Moore, 1779–1852

Arcane romantic flower, meaning what?
Do you know what it meant? Do I?
We do not know.
Unfolding pungent Rose, the glowing bath
Of ecstasy and clear forgetfulness;
Closing and secret bud one might achieve
By long debauchery—
Except that I have eaten it, and so
There is no call for further lunacy.
In Springfield, Massachusetts, I devoured
The mystic, the improbable, the Rose.

Of four electric stars which shone
Weakly into my room, for there,
Drowning their light and gleaming at my side,
Was the incarnate star
Whose body bore the stigma of the Rose.
And that is all I know about the flower;
I have eaten it—it has disappeared.
There is no Rose.

Hasbrouck and the Rose, Phelps Putnam, 1894–1948

The wheel of time turns,
foretells the future
tells the past.

Turns in the sun
and in the shadow.
Turns through the long night.

Counts off the days
and the years
and all the epochs

gives us the signs,
the ones to live by
and those to die by.

Carries us up the ninefold path
shows us the nine precious gifts
brings us face to face with the gods

guides us in our perilous journeys
teaches us of demons
who preside over the darkness.

Brings us to the awesome
reckoning with the rose
on whose petals are inscribed

the book of years,
the eternal turning
towards our ends.

The Tun Wheel, Mayan, fifteenth century

If thou canst but thither,
There grows the flower of Peace,
The Rose that cannot wither,
Thy fortress and thy ease.

Peace, Henry Vaughan, 1622–1695

The fairest things have fleetest end,
   Their scent survives their close:
But the rose's scent is bitterness
   To him that loved the rose.

Daisy, Francis Thompson, 1859–1907

Each Morn, a thousand Roses brings, you say:
Yes, but where leaves the Rose of Yesterday?

Stanza 9, The Rubaiyat, Omar Khayyam, 1070–1123

Among the generations of the rose
That have been lost in time's old manuscripts,
I was to salvage one of them from its
Oblivion, one unmarked, unseen from those
Earlier things. Now destiny provides
Me with the gift of naming for the first
Time that one soundless flower, the rose, the last
One Milton chose and lifted to his eyes,
Not seeing it. O you, vermillion, white
Or yellow rose now a garden blurred,
You leave your past and magically depose
All memory, yet in lines you persist bright
With gold or blood or ivory, as conferred
To darkness in his hands, invisible rose.

A Rose and Milton, Jorge Luis Borges, 1899–1986

'Tis the last rose of summer,
  Left blooming alone;
All her lovely companions
  Are faded and gone;
No flower of her kindred,
  No rose-bud is nigh,
To reflect back her blushes,
  Or give sigh for sigh!

I'll not leave thee, thou lone one!
  To pine on the stem;
Since the lovely are sleeping,
  Go, sleep thou with them.
Thus kindly I scatter
  Thy leaves o'er the bed,
Where thy mates of the garden
  Lie scentless and dead.

So soon may *I* follow,
  When friendships decay,
And from Love's shining circle
  The gems drop away!
When true hearts lie wither'd,
  And fond ones are flown,
Oh! who would inhabit
  This bleak world alone?

'Tis the Last Rose of Summer, Thomas Moore, 1779–1852

I am dreaming of a death of jasmine
and the lips of consolation and the sea
I am dreaming of a birth of burnt coral
the sun a yellow rose in your hair.

Ghazal of the Vigil, John Italia, born 1948

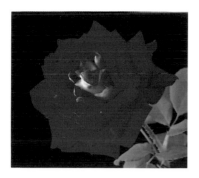

O, my Luve is like a red, red rose,
That's newly sprung in June.
O, my Luve is like the melodie
That's sweetly play'd in tune.

A Red, Red Rose, Robert Burns, 1759–1796

Why is it no one ever sent me yet
One perfect limousine, do you suppose?
Ah no, it's always just my luck to get
    One perfect rose.

One Perfect Rose, Dorothy Parker, 1892–1967

They are not long, the days of wine and
    roses;
Out of misty dream
Our path emerges for a while, then
    closes
Within a dream.

Vitae Summa Brevis Spem Nos Vetat Incohare Longam, Ernest Dowson, 1867–1900

note picture repositions as shown